GW00367600

Introduction

This book follows on from Book 4 - 'Creative Ide
expanding on the applications of some of the pr
ORCHARD PRODUCTS range and introducing
show the usual ORCHARD PRODUCTS flair for unique detail.
Some of the techniques referred to are described in detail in the previous books in this series (Books 1 to 4). A comprehensive index to all the books is included.
Glue. Throughout this book reference is made to 'glue', which is intended to mean Triple strength Rose Water or Gum Arabic. Egg white may be used if required.

The Tools. General Notes:

Non-stick. One of the most useful aspects of their design is their non-stick property which is inherent in the material used. It is not a surface finish and, therefore, cannot wear off.
Materials. All the tools can be used with any soft material such as flowerpaste, sugarpaste, marzipan, modelling chocolate, plasticine, modelling clay etc.
Temperature. They will withstand boiling water or the dishwasher without deforming.
Handles. All the cutters have comfortably sized hollow handles which allow you to exert firm pressure over the whole of the cutting edges.
Stability. They will not rust, corrode, deform or wear out with normal useage.
Marking. All the tools are permanently marked to aid easy identification.
Metal. They should not be brought into contact with sharp metal objects which may damage the cutting edges or surfaces i.e. keep them separated from metal cutters.
Boards. Our non-stick boards (white or green) with their rubber feet and non-stick rolling pins (5" to 23") really do make handling sticky materials more of a pleasure and enable you to roll out your pastes much thinner than you thought possible.
Hygiene. The materials meet the appropriate EEC regulations for food hygiene.
Endorsement. All the items are personally endorsed and used by PAT ASHBY, our Technical Director, who is one of the leading teachers of sugarcraft in the UK and is an International Judge.

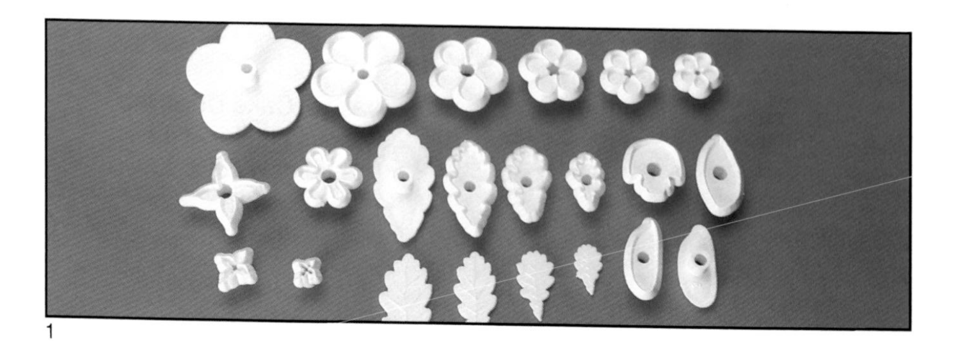
1

THE NEW CUTTERS (See Illustration 1).
(Full size shapes are shown in Illustrations 2 & 3).

1. The Five-petal Cutters (F7, F8, F9, F10). One of the most useful cutter types we have introduced is what we now call 'The Five-petal Flower' and in this book we show four more of the type, making a complete range of six cutters (F5-F10) from 65mm ($2\frac{1}{2}''$) to 20mm ($\frac{3}{4}''$), with which a complete spray of Roses (or other flowers) can be made quickly. The secret of their success are the long cuts in towards the centre, which separate the petals.

2. The Orchid Cutters (Cymbidium) Orchidee (OR1, OR2, OR3, OR4). These cutters have been copied exactly from real flowers and therefore contain one or two subtleties not found elsewhere, which should help you to produce botanically correct flowers.

3. The Daphne Cutters (D1, D2). These delightfully shaped cutters enable you to produce some pretty filler flowers easily. Follow the instructions for the throat carefully.

4. The Fuchsia Cutters (FS1, FS2). These colourful flowers can be produced quite quickly using these shapes and the advice given in this book.

5. The Oak Leaves & Veiners (OL1, OL2, OL3, OL4, OL5, OL6, OL7, OL8). These leaves complement many flowers and can form a colourful display of their own, as you can see from the illustration in the book.

Illustration 2 (Full size)

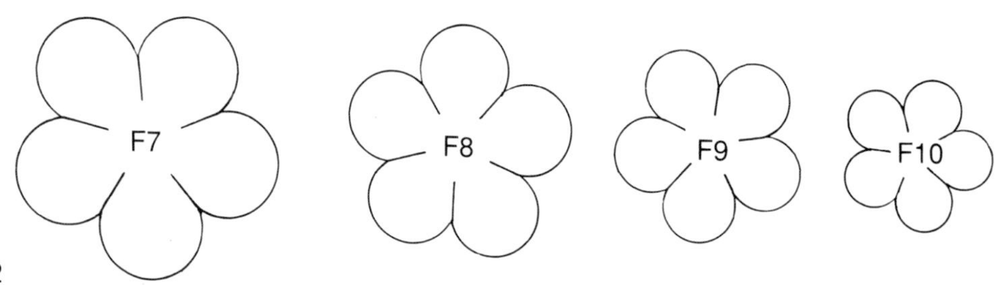

Illustration 3 (Full size)

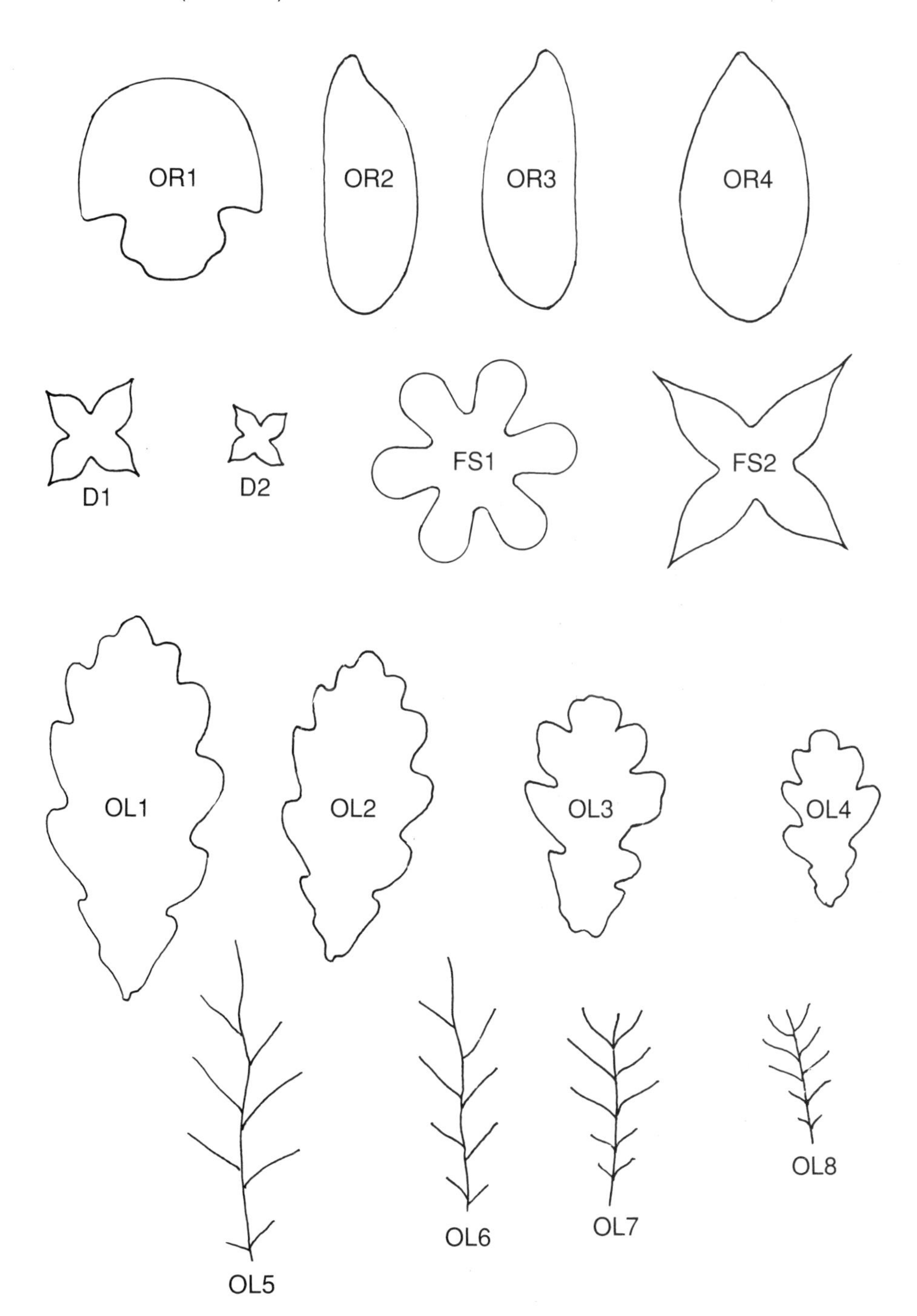

How to make the Azalea (See Illustration 4).

1. Wire 10 short stamens and one long stamen (stigma) to a 28 gauge wire Curve to shape (See Illustration 5). Moisten the end of the stamens with rose water and roll a tiny piece of white flowerpaste around the base. Leave to dry.
2. Make a Mexican hat with white flowerpaste using the Mexican Hat Adaptor (M1) – see Book 7 and cut out one Five-petal flower (F6). Since you will want to work on the shape for some little time grease the board and lightly grease the surface of the paste (this allows you to work without the paste drying too quickly).
3. Place the Mexican Hat shape on the Orchard Pad (PD1) and flap up each alternate petal. Soften the edges with the balling tool (OP1). This way you can soften right round the cut edge.
4. Place onto a non-stick board and frill the edges with a Frilling Tool (FT1). Place each petal on your forefinger in turn and roll across with the veining tool (OP2) (See Page 6). Indent petal 1 right down the centre.
5. Push the veining tool into the throat and press out against your finger to widen the throat. Glue the base of the stamens and thread the wire through the throat. The curved stamens should be facing No. 1 petal which has the groove.
6. Arrange the petals so that No. 1 petal overlaps petals 2 and 5. No. 3 overlaps No. 2 and No. 4 overlaps 5 and 3. Pop 'Cloud drift' under the petals for support so that they can curl naturally. All the petals curl under.
7. The stigma curves up facing No. 1 petal. This petal has painted marks on it, tiny dots growing into brush strokes. These come from the centre to one third of the way up, and there are a few similar marks on the inside edge of petals 2 and 5 (See Illustration 4). Petal dust the centre pink, fading towards the edges. Deeper pink veins appear on the back. When the flowers first appear they are very pink. As the flowers mature the colour becomes much lighter. Dust with plum petal dust. Paint the base of the flower with a small green circle.

How to make the Azalea Leaves (See Illustration 4).

1. Roll out green fowerpaste slightly thicker than usual and cut out a circle and then a segment (See Illustration 6). Mark the veins with a rose leaf veiner (R8, 9 or 10) by pressing with the Orchard Pad (PD1), thinning out the leaf except for a small area at its base.
2. Glue the end of a 26 gauge wire and holding the base between your finger and thumb push the wire into the thickened end of the leaf. Turn leaf over and soften the edges with a balling tool (OP1). Dry over a gently curved surface.
3. Tape the leaf wires to a 24 gauge wire, leaving a short stem, in layers of 3 leaves. Tape a second layer of 3 under the first but positioned between the leaves of the first layer.

4

5

6

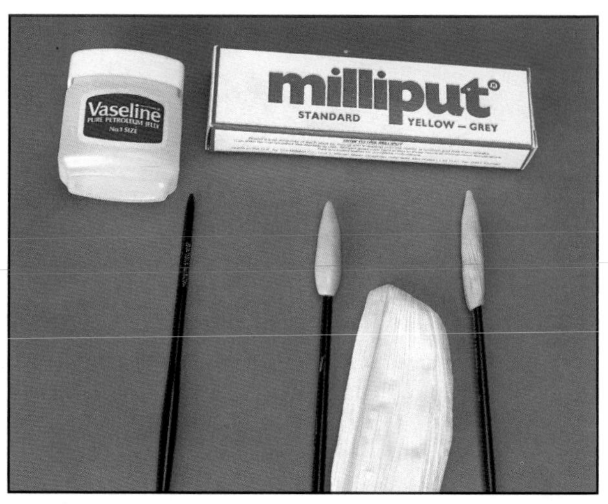

7

How to make the Veining Tool (See Illustration 7).

1. This very useful tool is simple to make, although there is a manufactured version now available (OP2). See Book 6.
2. Apply a little Vaseline to your hands to prevent sticking. Mix a small quantity of the two components of 'Milliput' epoxy resin (as described in Book 2 Page 29) and shape into an elongated cone. Push the end of an old paint brush handle into the cone and reshape the cone by rolling it between your hands.
3. Then, while still soft, wrap some dried corn husk round it, press in, remove and leave for a few hours to set hard.

How to make the Quick wired Rose (See Illustration 8).

1. Make a small hook on the end of a piece of 26 gauge wire and fit a small cone of coloured flowerpaste onto it with rose water. The cone should be shorter and slimmer than the size of the petal to be used. Leave to dry in the Flowerstand (S1) see Book 7.

N.B. Alternatively push the wire into a block of polystyrene for support or you can make a very effective flowerholder by pushing holes into the polystyrene with a paintbrush handle and then insert short pieces of drinking straw.

2. Roll out flowerpaste and cut out one shape F5 (or any of the five-petal cutters). Soften the edges of the petals with the balling tool (OP1)- bend up the petals either side so that you actually soften right the way down the cut edge. Place the shape onto a cornflour dusted sponge and circle each petal with the balling tool to cup and shape. Press into the centre.(See Illustration 9).
3. Glue the cone all round and thread through the centre of the shape. Wrap Petal 1 around the cone (See Illustration 10).

8

9

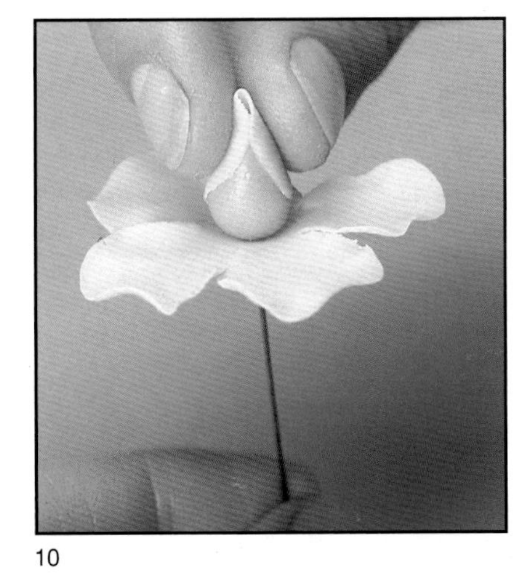

10

Wrap Petal 3 opposite Petal 1 leaving out Petal 2 (See Illustration 11 and Diagram 10A). Come back to Petal 2 and using the edge of petal No. 3 as a guide place this into the centre of Petal No. 2. Put a little glue on the side edge of Petal 2 and wrap round a little higher leaving the end free. Glue the back of Petal 3 and tuck the edge of Petal 4 inside Petal 2. Squeeze together leaving the outside edge of Petal 4 free. Glue Petal 2 to outside of Petal 4 (See Illustration 12). Glue the back of Petal 3 and tuck the edge of Petal 5 inside Petal 4. Glue inside of Petal 4 onto Petal 5. Glue outside edge of Petal 2 and wrap Petal 5 on top, so that the last three petals interleave. (See Illustration 13).

At this stage the flower should be allowed to dry a little before proceeding to the next stage. These five petals form a bud.

4. Repeat step 2 for the second set of petals. Put a little glue onto the bud and thread the wire through the centre of the shape (See Illustration 14). Using the edge of any petal as a guide place this into the centre of the first petal. All five petals of this set interleave (See Illustration 15).

5. Repeat Step 2 for the third set of petals. Turn the paste over onto a cornflour dusted sponge and press in the centre with the balling tool (OP1) (See Illustration 16). Place a little glue onto the base of the 2nd set of petals, thread the wire through the centre of the shape and push up so they fit snugly underneath the 2nd set of petals. Apply glue to each petal in turn. This third set of petals are set lower (See Illustration 17).

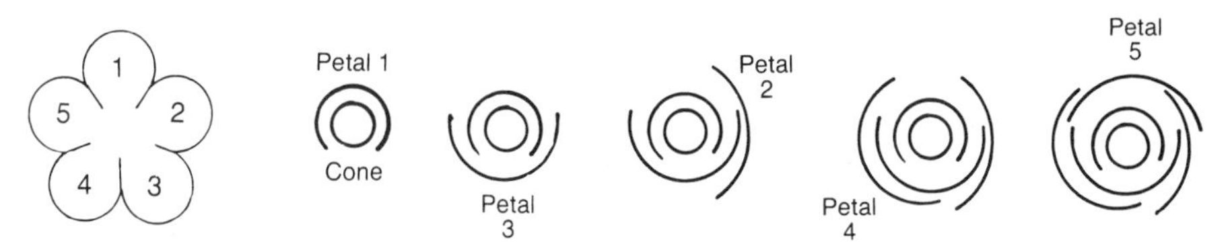

Diagram 10A

11

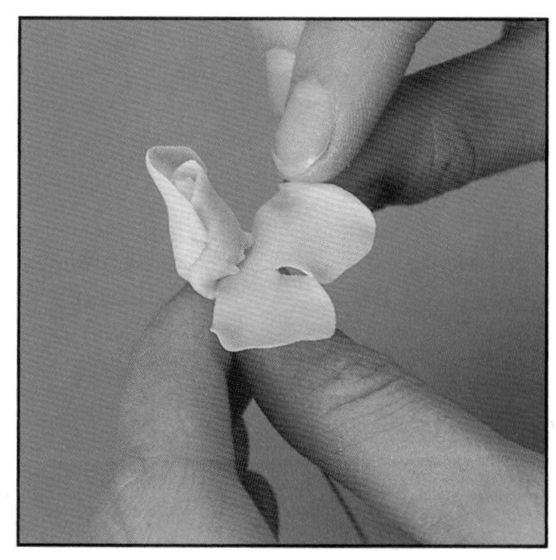

12

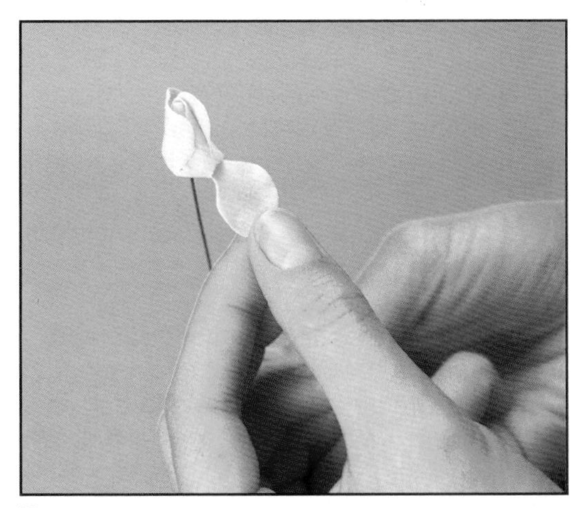

13

14

15

16

17

6. The Calyx. Roll out some green flowerpaste and cut out a calyx (R11). Cup by pressing with the balling tool (OP1) on the Orchard Pad (PD1) from the tips of the sepals towards the centre. Glue the base of the flower and thread the wire through the centre of the calyx so that it fits snugly. Put a small "golf tee' of green flowerpaste underneath for the hip and mark with a knife. Leave to dry. Bend the top edges over slightly. When dry, if required, dust the edges of the petals with a contrasting colour petal dust on a sable brush.

How to make the Christmas Rose. (See Illustration 19).

1. Roll out flowerpaste and cut out one F6. Soften the edges with the balling tool (OP1) on the Orchard Pad (PD1) and ball each petal to a point in the centre. Roll the veining tool over each petal. Place into an apple container (See Illustrationn 18).
2. Position the petals as follows: Petals 1 and 3 lay on the bottom. Petal 2 overlaps Petals 1 and 3. Petal 4 overlaps Petal 3, and Petal 5 overlaps Petals 1 and 4. Prop to shape with cloud drift. Leave to set.
3. Pipe a bulb of green Royal Icing in the centre of the flower and insert yellow-headed stamens. When dry dust around the centre with green petal dust. Attach to cake or plaque with Royal Icing.

18

19

How to make the Christmas Decoration (See Illustration 19).

1. Roll out sugarpaste/pastillage and cut out one oval plaque (P4 or P5). Leave to dry.
2. Paint in the Fern with a 000 paintbrush and edible colour. Leave to dry.
3. Make Christmas Roses as on Page 10.
4. Cut out Holly (H1, H2, H3, H4) and vein with the rose veiners (R8,R9,R10). (More details can be found in Book 3 Page 11.)
5. Cut out Ivy (IV1, IV2, IV3, IV4) and vein with the rose veiners. (More details can be found on Page 36 or in Book 3 Page 18.)
6. The candle is made from marzipan or sugarpaste.
7. Assemble with a little Royal Icing.

Understanding Colour.

(This section reproduced by kind permission of Vivian Ride and Betty Debnam of Tasmania.)

(This short article is intended to draw the readers attention to the significant effect colour can have in Cake Decorating, and to give some idea how these effects can be manipulated.)

Colour Theory. A **Colour Wheel** is an invaluable aid for gaining a full appreciation of the many possibilities for mixing primary, secondary and intermediate colours. (See Illustration 20).

1. The three basic or **primary** colours are red, yellow and blue.
2. The three **secondary** colours are formed by mixing any two primary colours, e.g.

   red + yellow = orange
   red + blue = purple
   yellow + blue = green
3. Intermediate colours are made by mixing a primary and its adjacent secondary colour to give more subtle shades, e.g. yellow/green or yellow/orange.
4. Harmonious colours are adjacent to each other on the colour wheel. These colours harmonize.
5. Each colour on the Colour Wheel has a **Complementary** colour directly opposite it.

   e.g.the Complementary colour of Red is Green.

   They are referred to as Complementary because they are enhanced when placed next to each other.
6. By mixing any two complementary colours together you will get varying shades of Brown, and by mixing all colours together you will (in theory) create Black.

Colour Theory in relation to Food Colours.

7. Many of the primary colours we use in cake decorating are not true primaries, e.g.

   Some 'Reds' have yellow added so when they are mixed with Blue they create a very muddy Purple.
8. Cake decorators rarely work with pure bright colours, and in wedding cakes for example we usually prefer quite pale colours.

   To lighten (or tint) colours use water or white modelling paste.

   To darken(or shade) a colour either add Black or the complementary colour.
9. Leaf Colours. Observation can make us aware that Nature is full of variety, and leaves are no exception. Our 'Leaf Green' colour is sometimes very inadequate.

   A more realistic base colour can be made by adding either Black, Brown or its Complementary which is Red.

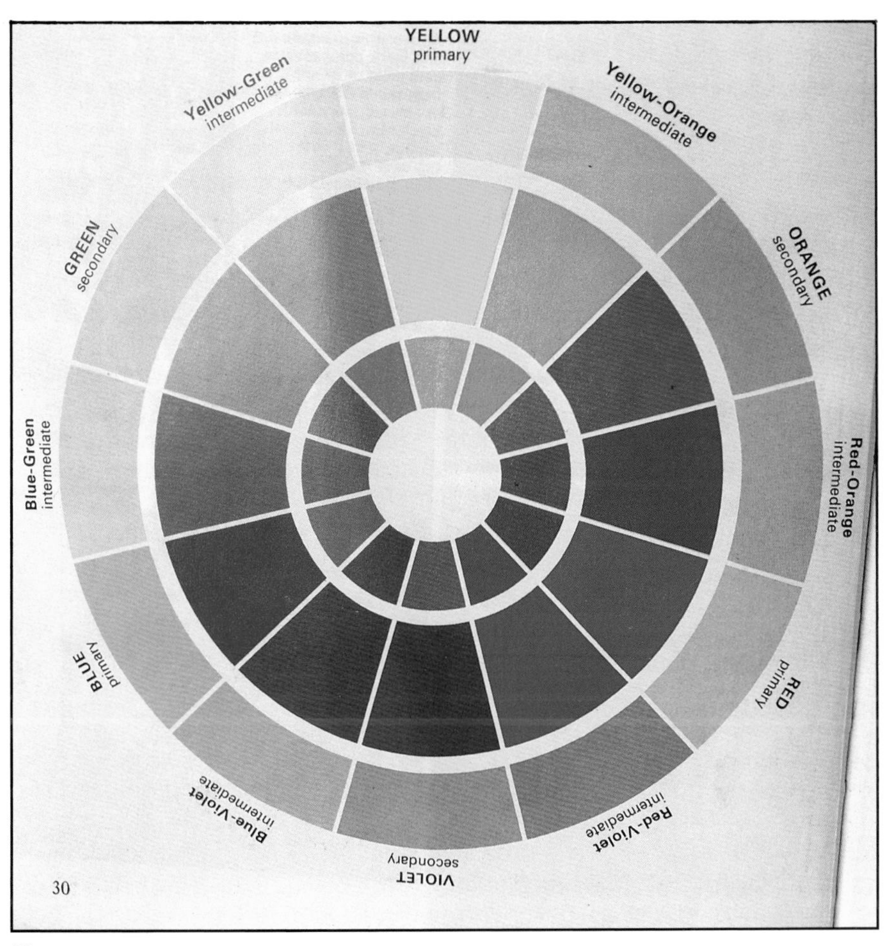

20

Base Green + Black for Holly and Ivy.
"   " + Yellow for young or variegated leaves.
Base Green + Blue for Carnation leaves
"   " + Red for Rose leaves

Leaves look more realistic if the colour is diluted with either pure alcohol (95%) and Rose Water (5%) OR water. This creates a more translucent effect, which is enhanced by 'steaming' them when dry. (See Page 16).

Colour Relationships.

10. Colour does not exist in isolation and will apparently vary according to the colour placed beside it. Your awareness of this relationship will develop through observation and experimentation.

Start by observing the Illustations 21 & 22. The centre colour in each of the three samples are the same!

Try placing a spray of flowers against different coloured backgrounds and note the effect. You will see why it is important to refer back to your cake colour when wiring together a spray. Experiment with different combinations of flowers, ribbons and leaves.

The Qualities of Colour.

Colours can be:

combined in either a harmonious or a contrasting arrangement.

Harmonious colours are adjacent to each other on the colour wheel, while contrasting colours are on opposite sides of the colour wheel.

Either warm or cool. As a general rule, warm colours tend to advance and cool colour tend to recede (this can be used very effectively when combining flowers in a spray).

Light or dark in tone. Light colours usually make objects look bigger and dark colours make objects look smaller - so the colour of your cake covering will effect the appearance of your cake.

By mixing light and dark coloured flowers together, your arrangement will appear more dynamic and dramatic.

Either Light or Dark colours grouped together will create a more harmonious and gentle arrangement.

Design Tips:

Next time you are designing a cake, you might find the following guidelines a useful aid.

1. Work with a limited number of colours until you gain confidence. I have found that working in odd numbers of flowers e.g. 3, 5, or 7 gives balance to your design. It is equally satisfying when used to arrange flowers in a spray.

2. Choose a main colour for your cake and then find suitable colours to support your colour theme.The choice will depend on whether you want it to be harmonious or dramatic.

3. Virtually any colours can be used together, providing there is repetition of these colours within the cake design. If incorporated within the floral decoration, ribbon, cake covering or board they will create a sense of balance.

21

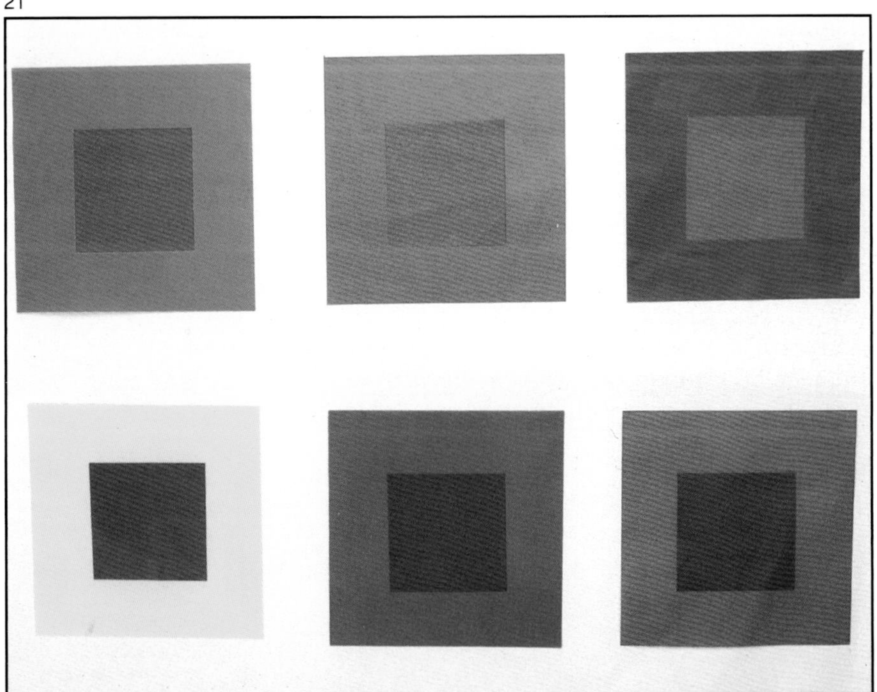
22

Colour Hints:
1. Food colours vary considerably between brands, so you will need to experiment for best results. Orchard Products dusting and paste colours are among the best.
2. Because artificial light can give a false idea of colour, it is better to colour in natural light.
3. There are two general rules for mixing colours:
For a light colour start with the lighter colour of the mix.
For a darker shade start with the darker colour of the mix.
Remember that it only takes a microscopic amount of black to change white to grey.

'Steaming' Flowers.
This simple technique gives sugar flowers a delightful translucent sheen and also blends surface colours together to give a more natural look. Just gently twirl the flower or leaf in the steam from a boiling kettle for 2 or 3 seconds. Repeat until the desired effect is achieved.

How to make the Large Primrose (See Illustration 23).
1. Tape one pale yellow stamen to the end of a piece of 26 gauge wire and using rose water or gum arabic as glue, attach a small piece of yellow flowerpaste to the bottom of the stamen.
2. Make a "Mexican Hat" of yellow flowerpaste using the Mexican Hat Adaptor (M1) see Book 7 and with the Large Primrose cutter (F4), cut out a flower complete with throat (See Illustration 24). Roll each section of the petal with a veining tool (See Page 6). Push the veining tool down into the centre and press against your finger to widen the throat.
Apply a little glue to the paste on the wire and push the wire into the throat until the end of the stamen is just below the opening in the centre.
3. Roll out green paste thinly and cut out a Medium Calyx (R12).
Cut off 2 sepals, cut down the centre of two adjacent sepals and spread out. Ball towards the centre with the balling tool (OP1) to cup, and vein with the veining tool (see Page 6).
Apply a little glue to the base of the flower and wrap the calyx round.
Dust the centre of the flower with egg yellow petal dust on a '0' sable brush.
N.B: The Small Primrose is described in Book 2 Page 16.

How to make the Primrose Leaves (See Illustration 23).
1. Using a reverse primrose leaf mould, made as directed on Page 30 of Book 2, make the leaf as directed on Page 31. Dry over the end of a wooden spoon to obtain the curved effect. Bend to the required shape before completely dry.

23

24

How to make the Minature Briar Rose (See Illustration 25).

1. Make a small hook in the end of a piece of 28/30 gauge wire and bend the hook over to one side.
2. Roll out white flowerpaste and cut out one flower using the large primrose cutter (F4). Place onto the Orchard Pad (PD1) and soften the edges with a balling tool (OP1).
3. Turn the flower over and ball just under the edge of each petal, which will make it cup. Turn over again, and curve all the petals up by pressing gently with the balling tool from centre of petal to centre of flower, taking care not to lose the shape on the cupped edge (See Illustration 26).
4. Apply glue to the hook and thread the rose onto the wire, making sure it is firmly pressed into the centre of the flower. Leave to dry in a suitable container.

5.Stamens. Cut approx. 12/15 yellow stamens to unequal lengths. Add a little rose water to some pale yellow flowerpaste (to make it a little softer and stickier). Take a tiny ball of this paste, flatten slightly, dampen centre of rose with glue and press in the ball. Alternatively use Yellow Royal Icing. Insert the longer stamens, with tweezers, into the ball N, S, E & W with the shorter ones in between making sure the effect is kept uneven. Keep the centre clear.

6. The Caiyx. Roll out some green flowerpaste and cut out a calyx (R13). Cup by balling with the balling tool (OP1) on the Orchard Pad (PD1) from the tips of the sepals towards the centre. Glue the base of the flower and thread the wire through the centre of the calyx so that it fits snugly. Small ball of green paste for the hip. Glue the centre of the calyx and thread the wire through the centre of the ball and press gently to the base of the calyx. Leave to dry. When dry dust the edges of the petals with rose coloured petal dust and the centre yellow.

25

26

How to make the Poached Egg Flower (See Illustration 27.)

1. Hook a 28/30 gauge wire and bend the hook over.
Roll out white flowerpaste and cut out one shape (F4). Soften the petals with a balling tool (OP1) on the Orchard Pad (PD1) and roll each section of the petals with a veining tool (OP2). Press and circle the balling tool (OP1) in the centre to cup the flower. Glue the hooked end of the wire and slide down the centre of the flower. Leave to dry in a suitable container (See Illustration 28) like the Flowerstand (S1) – see Book 7.
2. When dry paint lemon yellow on the petals using a No. 1 paintbrush and long strokes. Turn over and paint the back. Leave to dry. For quicker drying time use alcohol instead of water.
3. When dry pipe a small amount of yellow Royal Icing into the centre and push in I0 yellow tipped stamens.
4. Calyx. Roll out green flowerpaste and cut one calyx (R13), soften the edges, glue and thread up through the base to fit snugly around the flower.
5. Small Bud. Make a green flowerpaste cone. Glue the end of a 30 gauge wire and thread through the centre of the cone. Mark cone to form calyx with the back of a knife.
6. Large Bud. Make a white flowerpaste cone. Glue the top of a 30 gauge wire and push into the base of the cone. Leave to dry. When dry paint lemon yellow around the lower half of the bud (See Illustration 28). Leave to dry.
7. Roll out green flowerpaste and cut out a tiny calyx (R15). Glue the base of the bud and thread wire into centre of the calyx to cup around the base. Leave to dry.

27

28

29

How to make the Fabric covered board (See Illustration 30).
Choose a soft fabric such as chiffon, silk, lace or polyester, in a suitable colour. Cut out a circle 7.5cm (3") larger all the way round the board,i.e. for an 20cm(8") dia. board cut out 35cm (14") dia. fabric.
2. Using a long, double thread, run a gathering stitch around the fabric, 1cm ($\frac{1}{2}$") from the edge.
3. Place a cake board in the centre and draw the edges of the fabric together as tightly as possible. (See Illustration 29).
Tie the threads firmly and arrange the gathers evenly around the board.
Place a circle of greaseproof paper or thin cake card underneath the cake.
This technique is easiest on a round or oval board, but it can be fitted to other rounded shapes.

30

How to make Quilling. (See Illustration 30).

This is a new technique in sugarcraft, details not having been published before.

1. Quilling is also known as paper lace, paper filigree, or paper mosaic. It is the art of rolling thin strips of paper (or in our case flowerpaste) into various shapes and using the shapes to form designs. This type of filigree work has been found on ancient Egyptian, Greek and Etruscan tombs. It later became open work and was made of fine wires formed into lacy scrolls, arabesques and leaves. The shapes can be coiled into cones, scrolls, hearts, tear drops or leaf shapes. The coil can be pinched with tweezers at either end, or pressed either side with a knife to form either a square or a diamond shape.

2. Basic equipment is a cake board or polystyrene ceiling tile, 'easi-off' plastic, glass headed pins, parsley/mint cutter, large hat pin and a cocktail stick. For a three dimensional effect just build up the layers on top of the first set.

3. To commence work. (Templates 62, 63 & 64 on Pages 42 & 43).
Place design on top of cake board covered by plastic 'easi-off'. Stick or pin to the board (See Illustration 32).
Roll out flowerpaste and cut strips with your parsley cutter (See Illustration 31). Smear a little white fat over the surface and cover with plastic. This will give you plenty of time to work the paste before it dries out.
Commence with the main part of the design e.g. with the peacock start with the eyes and work out. With the Christmas design work from the centre outwards.
4. Take a strip of paste, lay it on a non-stick board and place either a hat pin (for finer coils) or cocktail stick flat on the paste, finger on top, roll over once and put on a little rose water to glue the first coil. If you want a tight coil, roll on and when you have reached the required size put a little rose water under the end. Pick this up (it can be moved with tweezers) and place onto the design, pushing a glass headed pin in the centre of the coil. Should you require the coil to be wide and loose, push a hat pin into the centre of the coil and commence uncoiling it with an anti-clockwise motion. When you have produced the desired effect, pin each section. Always glue closed coils before pinching them into other shapes (See Illustration 32).
5. Make another shape adjacent to the first and glue together with rose water. You can highlight various sections by placing a plain strip of light brown paste between each section. Assemble the design while it is still soft. It can be left on the board until dry and then moved while still on the plastic to the cake. Remove plastic and stick to the cake with rose water or a little Royal Icing.
6. Ideas you can make with quilling are birds, animals, owls, butterflies, flowers, faces, boxes (See Illustrations 33, 34 & 35).
Think of your filigree and piped chocolate designs. The ideas are endless.

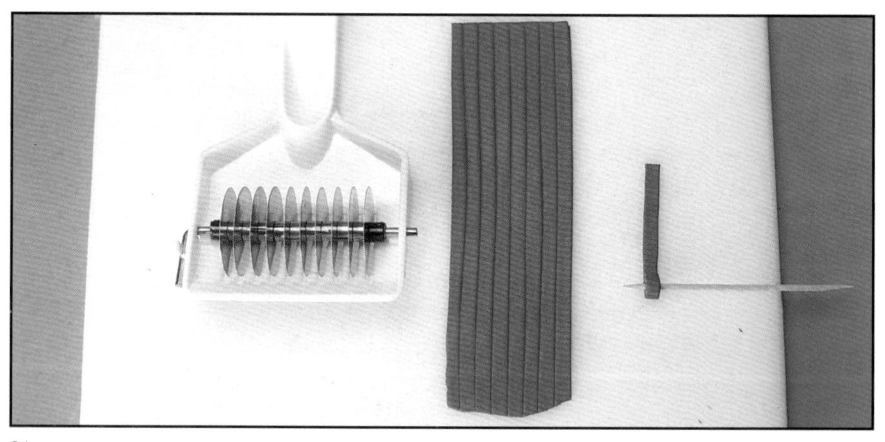

31

32

33

34

35

36

How to make the Cymbidium Orchid (See Illustration 36).
As with all flowers it is always better, if at all possible, to have a real flower in front of you to copy. The photographs are a reasonable substitute.
1. Column. This must be made 24 hours in advance to ensure that it is thoroughly dry.
Roll a pea sized piece of modelling paste into a ball, and then into a sausage tapered at one end. The length should be down to the first curve on the labellum (OR1) (See Illustration 37).
Curve slightly and hollow out the inside of the curve with the balling tool (OP1). Curve a piece of white 28 gauge wire, glue the end and, holding the column between finger and thumb, push the wire into the thick end of the column.
2. 'Colour code' the end of the wire, say orange, with a felt tip pen.
3. Roll a tiny piece of paste into a sausage and mark across the centre with the back of a knife to make 2 'eyes'. Glue to the top of the column.
4. Labellum. Roll out the flowerpaste and cut out the labellum (OR1). Soften the edges with the balling tool (OP1) and gently frill the front of the labellum with a cocktail stick. Make two ridges in the centre with a pair of tweezers commencing from the back to the first curve. Shape to an open V. Alternatively glue two small sausages of paste in the centre.
5. Apply glue to the back of the column and 1/3rd of the sides and attach it to the top of the labellum. The front of the labellum curves down. Leave to dry. Because this orchid is relatively small it does not need a former for support.
(Page 29) *'Cloud drift' is Acrylic fibre material teased out, as used in duvets.

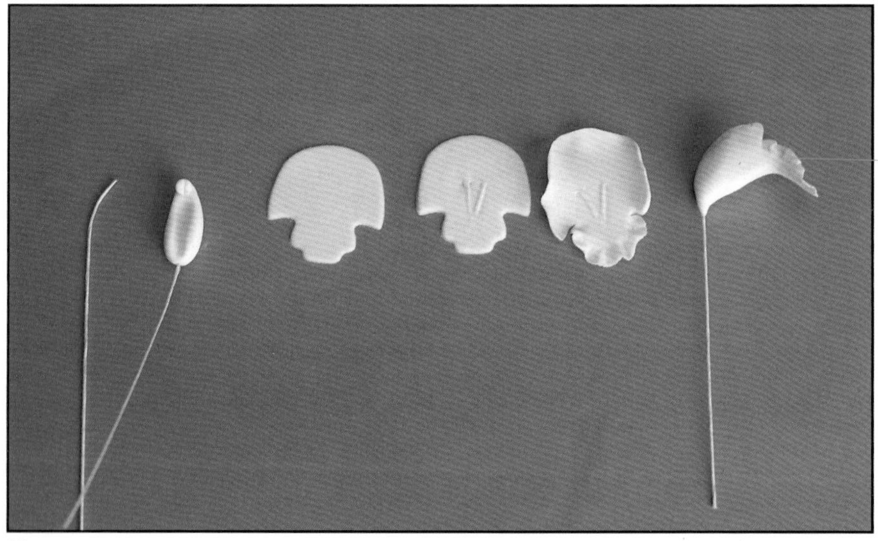

37

6. Sepals. (3 required). Roll out the flowerpaste leaving a thickened end for the base of the sepal. Cut out one sepal (OR4). Soften the edges. Roll veining tool over the top and mark centre vein. Pinch in the top of the sepal. Insert a glued 28 gauge wire into the thickened end.
Place in a curved position on a corrugated piece of plastic to dry. Prop with *'Cloud drift' (See Illustration 38 - No.1).
7. Repeat step 6 for two more sepals, but, this time hold the base between your finger and thumb and bend the wire until it hangs straight down over the edge (See Illustration 38 - No's 2 & 3). For easier assembly 'colour code' the base of the wires as for step 2, say red,white & blue.
8. Petals. Roll out the flowerpaste and cut out one each (OR2-left & OR3-right). Soften the edges and vein with the veining tool. Insert the glued end of a 28 gauge wire into the thickened end of the petal. Leave to set over the corrugated plastic in a slightly curved position. Hold the base between your finger and thumb and bend the wire until it hangs straight down over the edge (See Illustration 38 - No's 4 & 5). 'Colour code' the wires, say yellow & green.
9. Assembly. The reason for 'colour coding' will now become apparent. Instead of taping all the wires together immediately under the flower and then trying to adjust the positions of the components, place the three sepals (OR4) together to form a propeller shape. Place a petal (OR2 & OR3) either side of the top sepal and pop the labellum (OR1) in the centre. Carefully start taping the wires together about 1" below the base of the flower and continue taping for another 1".
10. Then carefully pull the top sepal (red) down to the tape and repeat for the other sepals,petals and labellum in the sequence shown in Diagram 39. Arrange the orchid artistically and then continue taping to the end of the wire.
11. Colouring. Colour and petal dust each specimen. For a pollen effect on the column and grooves on the labellum they can be glued and then brushed with coloured caster sugar, semolina, ground rice or mealie meal. Remember that the colouring makes the Orchid.

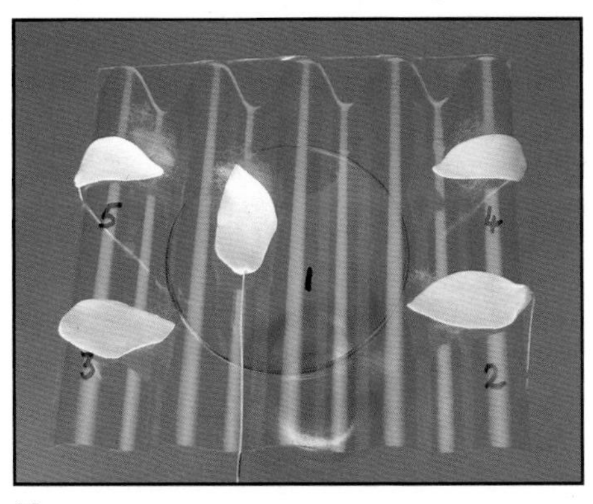

38

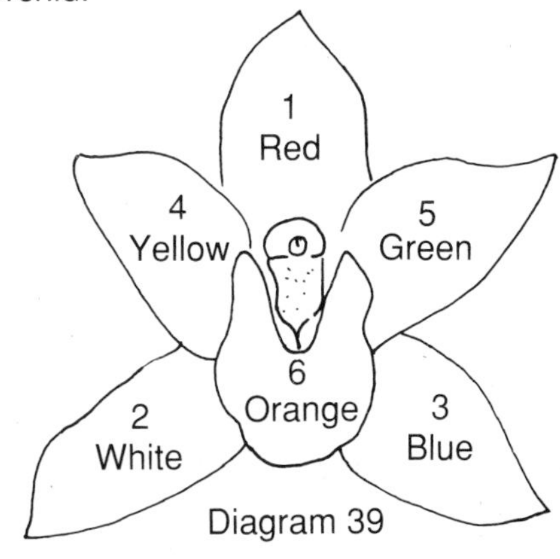

Diagram 39

40

41

How to make the Mini Orchid (See Illustration 40).

1. Column. Make a tiny sausage tapered at one end. Groove the centre with a tiny balling tool or glass-headed pin. The length of the column is the same as from the top of the labellum to the first cut (See Illustration 42). Glue the end of a curved 30 gauge wire and thread it through the thick end of the sausage. Leave to set.
2. Roll out flowerpaste and cut out one labellum (R18). Cut out a triangle either side of the petal (See Illustration 42). Make two indentations in the shape of an open triangle with a fine pair of tweezers. Soften the top edges with a balling tool where you have made the cuts and frill the remainder of the labellum with a cocktail stick. Put a little glue on the sides of the column and press the labellum onto it. The front turns down in a curve. Leave to dry.
3. Roll out the same colour flowerpaste and cut out one calyx shape (R13). Soften the edges with the balling tool and ball four sepals towards the centre. Turn the piece over and ball the last sepal in the same manner. Place on a cornflour dusted sponge and press in the centre. Put a little glue on the back of the labellum and thread the wire through the centre of the calyx shape. Position the top sepal curving over the labellum and the remainder curving back (See Illustration 41).
4. When dry, paint and dust to suit. These make very pretty filler flowers (See Illustration 41) or can be put into a miniature bouquet.

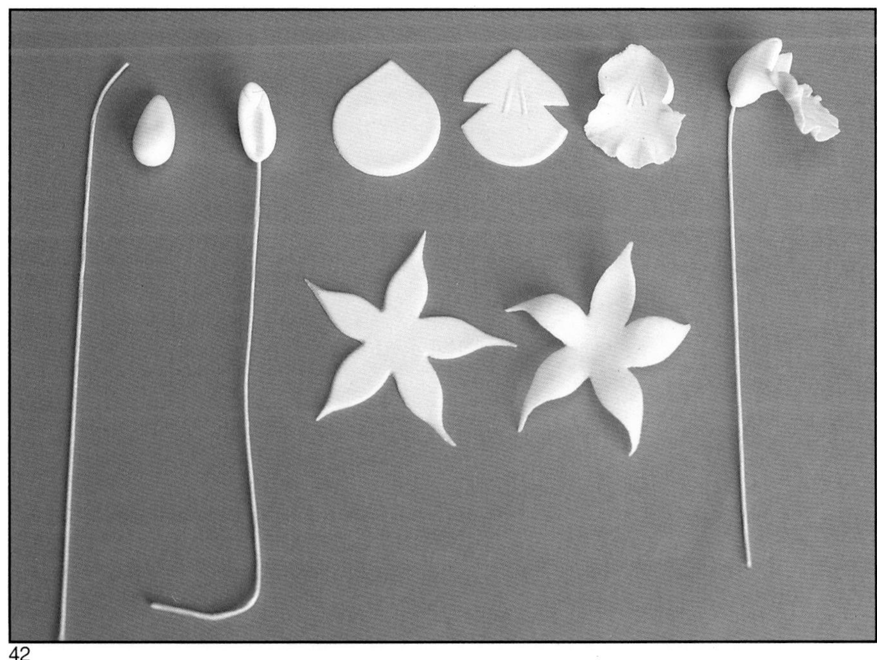

42

How to make a Mini wired Rose (using R15, R16, Rl7, R18 or F8) (See Illustration 43).

1. Glue a tiny cone of paste onto a 30 gauge wire. The cone should not be longer than the size of the petal to be used.
2. Roll out flowerpaste very thinly and cut out 2 petals with cutter (R18). Soften the edges slightly with the balling tool (OP1).
3. Apply a little glue to the first petal and fold right round the cone so that the centre cannot be seen.
4. Apply a little glue to the second petal and fold it opposite the first with the centre over the join of the first petal. Tip the top away from the centre and bend it back slightly (See Illustration 44).
5. Cut out 3 more (R18) petals, soften the edges and cup them slightly with the balling tool, keeping the prepared petals covered with plastic to stop them drying out too soon. Put a little glue on the side edge of the third petal and wrap round a little higher using the join of the second petal as a guide for the centre of the third petal leaving the unglued side open. Glue the back of Petal No. 2 and tuck in Petal No. 4. Glue open end of Petal 3 on outside of Petal 4. Repeat for Petal No. 5 so that the last three petals interleave (See Illustration 45).
6. Cut out 4 or 5 more petals and place these in the same fashion round the last three but slightly lower and bending the top edges over slightly. More petals can be added if desired.
7. Roll out green flowerpaste and cut out a small calyx using the Rl5 cutter. Ball lightly with the balling tool from the tips of the sepal to the centre. Glue the base of the rose and slide the calyx up the wire, until it folds round the base of the rose.
8. Put a small 'golf tee' of green flowerpaste underneath for the hip and mark with a knife. Leave to dry. When dry, if required, dust the edges of the petals with a deeper colour petal dust on a sable brush.

Rose Leaf.

Roll out green flowerpaste and leave a thickened piece in the middle. Cut out one leaf using (R16). Glue the end of a 30 gauge wire and holding the base of the leaf between finger and thumb push the wire a little way into the paste. Press on veiner (R17). Bend to shape. Leave to dry.

43

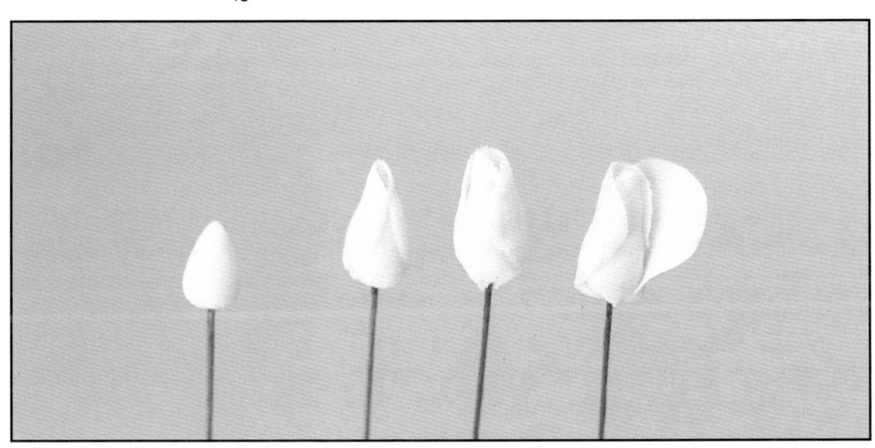

44

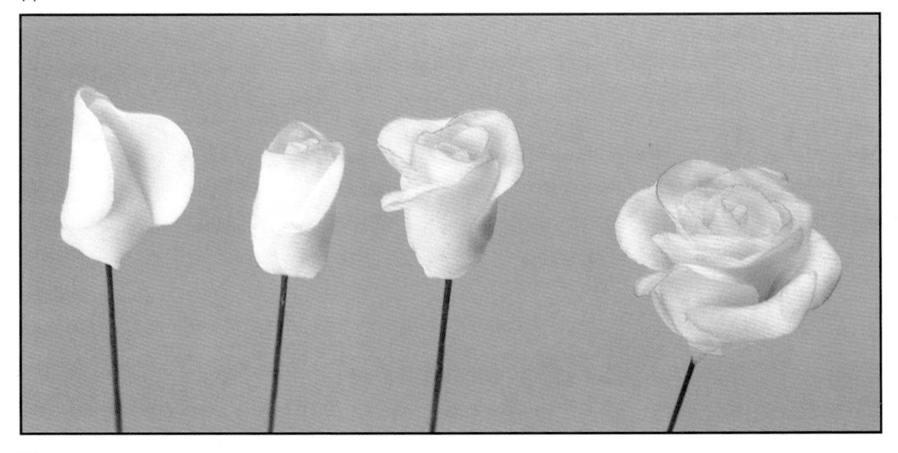

45

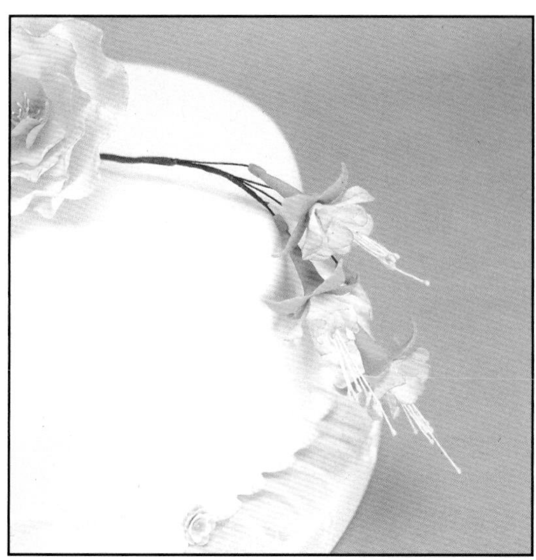

46

How to make the Fuchsia (See Illustration 46).

1. Wire 1 long stamen and 6 shorter stamens onto a 28 gauge wire by placing the wire beside and parallel to the stamens, and bending the top of the wire over and around the stamens two or three times. Moisten the base of the stamens with rose water and roll a small piece of paste onto the base. Leave to dry.
2. Roll out flowerpaste and cut out one FS1. Lay the shape onto a cornflour dusted board and frill alternate petals with a cocktail stick. Turn the paste over and frill the remaining petals.
Glue the paste at the base of the stamens and thread the wire through the centre of the petals. Press gently onto the base and leave upside down to dry a little (See Illustration 47).
3. Repeat step 2. Apply glue to the first set of petals about a quarter of the way up. Thread the wire through the second set of petals and line up the centre of one petal with the edge of one of the first petals. Press the base gently and leave upside down to dry.
4. Using the Calyx FS2 make a 'Mexican Hat' from flowerpaste with a slender top. Place the cutter over the centre and cut out the calyx. Soften the edges with the balling tool (OP1) and ball each sepal from the point to the centre. Press into the centre with the balling tool.
5. Moisten the centre of the calyx a quarter of the way up each sepal. Thread the flower into the centre and arrange around the flower. Roll the base of the calyx between finger and thumb to thin.
6. Roll a small ball of green flowerpaste. Moisten the base and thread the wire through the centre of the ball. Roll between finger and thumb to merge into the base. Curve wire to shape.

47

48

Bookstand (See Illustration 48).

This most useful device allows you to read your instruction book as you are doing the work, and only takes up 3" of your precious worktop space. It also keeps the books clean even with pointing sticky fingers!

It will hold any normal cake decorating or cookery book, hard or softback, and has no moving parts to go wrong.

49

50

51

How to make the Virginia Creeper (See Illustration 49).

1. Roll out red flowerpaste and cut out the required number and size of ivy leaves from IV1, IV2, IV3 or IV4. Soften the edges with the balling tool (OP1) on the Orchard Pad (PD1).
2. Mark the veins by pressing each leaf onto the appropriate sized Leaf Mould (R8, R9, RIO). Bend to shape and leave to dry.
3. Wired leaves (See Illustration 50). When making wired leaves leave a thickened piece in the centre and cut out the leaf. Soften the edges with the balling tool (OP1).
4. Dip the wire (28 gauge or smaller) into rose water. Holding the base of the leaf between finger and thumb wiggle the wire gently into the base. Vein onto the appropriate sized Leaf Mould (R8, R9, R10). Twist the leaf and leave to set.

Variegated Ivy (See Illustration 51).

Cut out a small ivy leaf of one colour paste and place on a larger piece of a different colour. Roll out and cut out a larger Ivy shape. Continue as above.

52

53

How to make the Daphne (See Illustration 52).

1. This is a quick way of making these flowers. Roll out flowerpaste and cut out several flowers (D1 and/or D2). Turn the paste over onto the Orchard Pad (PD1) and press out with the balling tool (OP1). Pick up a flower and in the centre of each petal mark one vein. Make a hole in the centre and leave to dry.
2. When dry, thread a stamen through the centre and glue with a little Royal Icing. Leave to dry (See Illustration 53).
3. Put a little glue in the middle of the stamen (under the petals) and roll a tiny piece of flowerpaste onto the stamen, rolling the paste between your finger and thumb until it is the correct shape (tubular) for the throat. Put a little rose water under the flower and slide up the base. Leave to set.
4. Dust the back and front of the flower mauve/pink and the base green. The Daphne makes a pretty filler flower (See Illustration 40) and can also be used as a blossom.

54

How to make the Oak Leaves (See Illustration 54).

1. Oak leaves can be made in various shades of green, orange, yellow and brown. They also look most attractive in white, edged with a pale colour to complement an artistic arrangement of flowers.
2. To obtain an Autumn shade, roll out sausages of flowerpaste in yellow, orange and green, press together, cut and repeat two or three times. Roll out the paste flat and cut out the autumn leaves (OL1, OL2, OL3, OL4). Vein with the veiners (OL5, OL6, OL7, OL8), then soften the edges with the balling tool (OP1). Twist to shape and leave to dry.

55

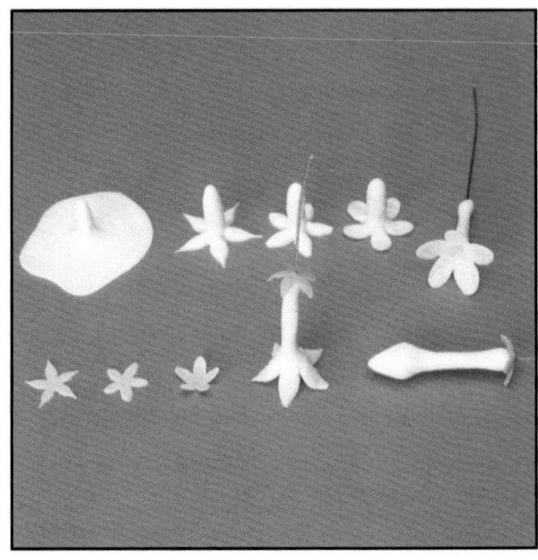

56

How to make the Stephanotis (See Illustration 55).

1. Stephanotis is a white 5 petal flower often used in bridal bouquets. Make a Mexican Hat using white flowerpaste using the Mexican Hat Adaptor (M1) see Book 7 and cut out one calyx (R13) and cut off the tips. Place the flower on the Orchard Pad (PD1), soften and widen each petal with a balling tool (OP1).
2. Hook a 26 gauge wire, glue the end and press through the centre of the flower. Roll the back between your fingers to thin out. The bottom of the base is rounded at the end. Make a hole in the centre of the flower with a knitting needle (See Illustration 56).
3. Vein each petal, using you veining tool (See Page 6).
i.e. lay the petal on your finger and roll the veining tool over the petal. Curl the petals to shape.
4. Calyx. Roll out green flowerpaste and cut out one calyx (R15). Cut off the tips and then soften the edges and in the centre of each sepal mark one vein. Push the wire through the centre of the calyx. Glue the bottom of the flower and push up to cup neatly at the base of your Stephanotis.
5. The flowers of the Stephanotis form clusters of 5 or 6. The leaves are dark green, oval in shape, smooth on the outside and the veins alternate.

Stephanotis leaves.
Roll out dark green flowerpaste and cut out one circle, as for the Azalea, (See Illustration 6). Come in with the cutter and cut out a leaf. Soften the edges with a balling tool (OP1) and vein on a rose veiner. For a large leaf start at the top of the leaf, press the veiner on the paste and then move the veiner down to complete the leaf. For a wired leaf moisten the end of a 28 gauge wire with rose water and holding the bottom of the leaf between finger and thumb gently ease the wire into the paste. Curve to shape.

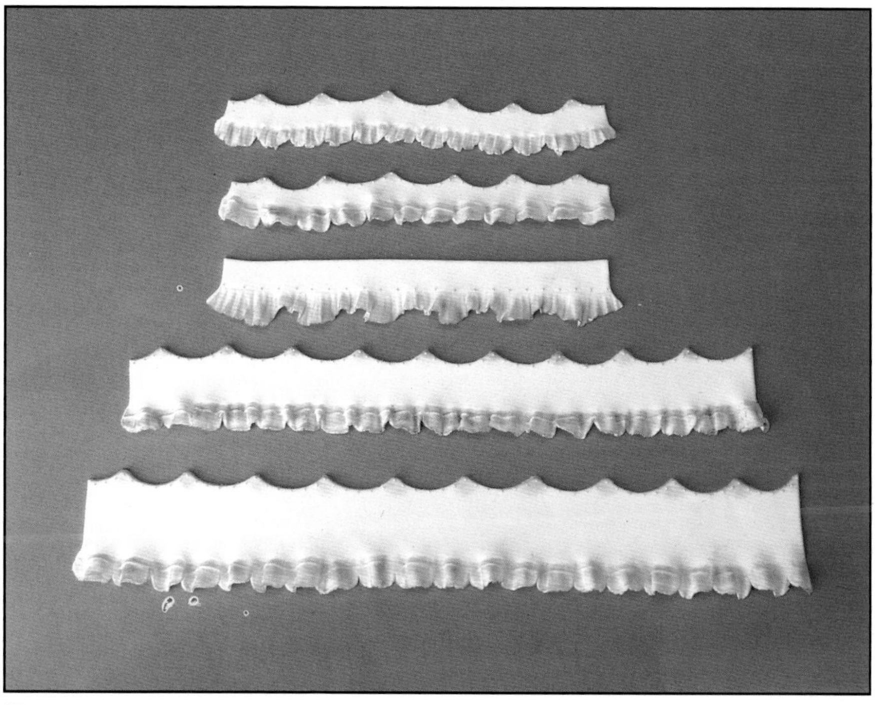

57

How to make the Endless Garrett Frill (See Illustrations 57, 58 & 59).
1. This unique cutter can produce 9 different styles of frill if you position either of the two detachable blades (EGF6 or 7) in the holes marked "Narrow" or "Medium" or "Wide". Thus any style (A, B or C) can be used for any width (See Diagram 61). (The widths correspond with the circular Garrett Frill Cutter (GF1, 2, 3, 4) described in Book 3). Since the cutter has no ends the frills can be of any length, simply by moving the cutter along and lining up carefully with the previous cutout. A cut with the straight blade (EGF6) or a knife then gives the exact length required. This is a great help for square cakes. It can also save time on a circular cake by allowing a continuous frill with only one join. Hint: 'Park' the unused blade in the spare holes on the handle side of the cutter.

2. The Garrett Frill cutter makes a very pretty border for a cake. It can also be used for dresses etc.
Roll out sugarpaste and dust your board with a little cornflour. This allows the paste to 'slide' as you frill it. (A new disposable nappy liner makes a very convenient bag for the cornflour).
3. Place a Frilling Tool (FT1 to 4) flat on the board with the tapered end over the edge of the paste. Rock the Frilling Tool back and forth one or two times with your forefinger, pressing firmly until the paste frills are as you require. Then move it along and repeat.
4. To make a shell-like frill press a cocktail stick either side of a flute making a triangular shape (See Illustration 60). See also Book 3.
Lay the cocktail stick down the centre and indent repeatedly from the centre out to the left keeping the end of the stick at the point of the triangle. Come back to the centre and repeat to the right. Make sure you give more pressure on the outside to make a finer edge. Do not press too hard otherwise the whole triangle will be cut out.
Continue in the same manner all round the Garrett Frill. This is most effective decoration and was shown to me by Rose Taylor of Zimbabwe.
Should you require a longer frill then just make a longer triangle.
A different effect can be achieved by using a grooved Frilling Tool. Attach the finished border to the cake with a little water. When dry dust with a little petal dust.

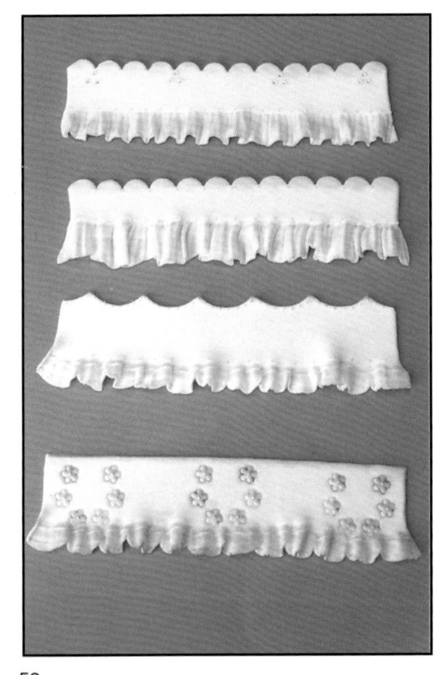

58

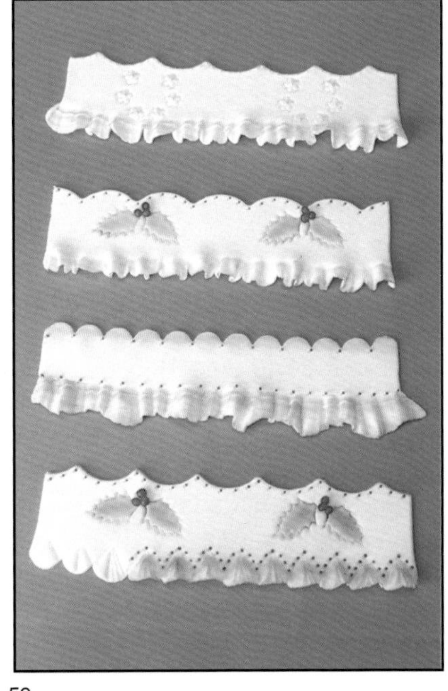

59

60

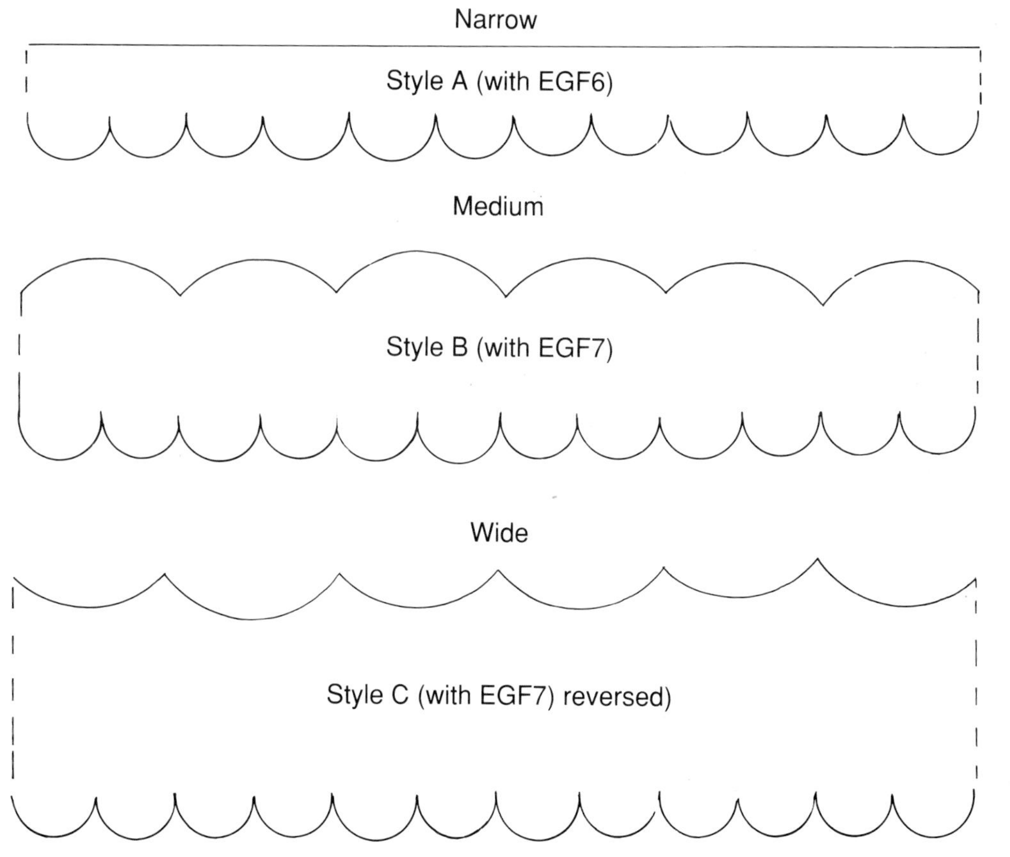

Diagram 61

Template 62

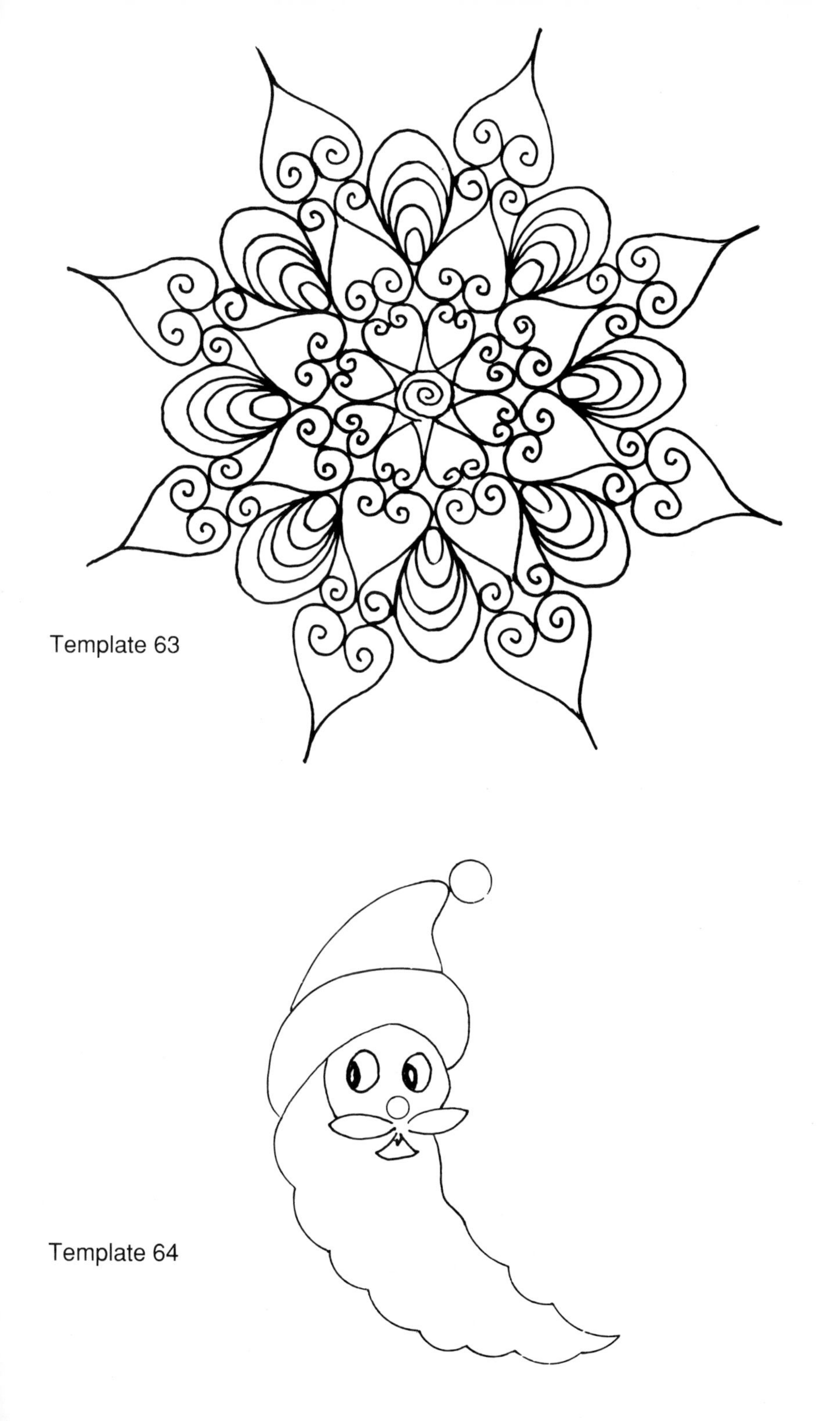

Template 63

Template 64

RECIPES

Flowerpaste A. 250g ($\frac{1}{2}$lb) Bakels 'Pettinice' or Craigmillars 'Pastello' **only**.
1 teaspoon Gum Tragacanth.

Rub 'Trex' on your hands and knead ingredients together until elastic. Wrap tightly in plastic and store in an airtight container. Leave for 24 hours. There is no need to refrigerate. This paste keeps well if worked through say, once a week. Always keep tightly wrapped.

Flowerpaste D. 450g sieved icing sugar
5mls Gum Tragacanth and 20mls Carboxymethyl Cellulose (CMC)
10mls powdered Gelatine soaked in 25mls of cold water
10mls white fat (Trex or Spry, not lard)
10mls liquid Glucose
45ml egg white

Sieve all the icing sugar into a greased* (Trex) mixing bowl. Add the gums to the sugar. Warm the mixture in a microwave oven - 3 x 50secs on medium setting - stirring in between.
Sprinkle the gelatine over the water in a cup and allow to sponge. Put the cup in hot, not boiling, water until clear. Add the white fat and liquid glucose. Heat the dough hook and add the dissolved ingredients and the egg white to the warmed sugar, and beat on the lowest speed until all the ingredients are combined. At this stage the mixture will be a dingy biege colour. Turn the machine to maximum speed and mix until the mixture becomes white and stringy. Grease your hands and remove the paste from the machine.
Pull and stretch the paste several times. Knead together and then cut into 4 sections. Knead each section again and place in a plastic bag, then in an airtight container and keep in the fridge.
Let it mature for 24 hours.
This paste dries very quickly so, when ready to use, cut off only a small piece and re-seal the remainder. Work it well with your fingers. It should be the consistency of well chewed chewing gum. If it should be a little too hard and crumbly, add a little egg white and white fat. The fat slows down the drying process and the egg white makes it more pliable.
Keep coloured paste in a separate container.

*This eases the strain on the machine considerably.

Pastillage.	Make up 8ozs of Royal Icing. Add 2 level 5ml teaspoons of Tylose. Mix well together. Wrap in cling film and place in an airtight container. Store in the fridge. Leave overnight before working

Gum Arabic Glue.
Use proportions of 3:1 of tepid water and Gum Arabic i.e. 3 teaspoons of water to 1 teaspoon of Gum Arabic. Place in a clean nail varnish container or similar and shake well.

COMBINED INDEX (for Books 1, 2, 3, 4 and 5).

All the items in this book can be obtained from your local sugarcraft retailer or by post from:-

Orchard Products
51 Hallyburton Road
Hove
East Sussex BN3 7GP
England
Tel: (0273) 419418
Fax: (0273) 412512

Photography by G. Ashby

Printed by Gemini Press Limited, Dolphin Way, Shoreham-by-Sea, West Sussex

There are other books by Pat Ashby in this series:-

'Blossoms to Bonzai' — Book 6
(ISBN 1 872573 06 1)

'Flowers and Favours' — Book 7
(ISBN 1 872573 07 X)

'The Orchard Lace Collection' — Book 8
(ISBN 1 872573 08 8)